PREGNA GUIDE FOR MEN

EVERYTHING YOU NEED TO KNOW ABOUT PREGNANCY AND WHAT TO DO IN THE NEXT 9 MONTHS

MATTHEW MUMFORD

TABLE OF CONTENTS

INTRODUCTION

Congratulations! You are about to embark upon a life-changing journey. This will change your perception of what it means to be a father. You will want to know many things as you prepare for your baby's birth. What should you do during your partner's pregnancy? What can you do to support your partner during this time? How can you prepare for your baby's arrival?

This book, "First Time Dad: Everything You Need to Know About Pregnancy and What to Do in the Next Nine Months," will answer all these questions and more. You can trust me to help you navigate this overwhelming and exciting time in your life. I will also share practical tips and advice to help you become a better dad.

The following pages will cover the main stages of pregnancy and childbirth. They start when you discover you will be a father to the day you give birth to your baby. You will learn about the emotional and physical changes your partner will experience during each trimester. I also offer tips on supporting her and participating in the pregnancy.

This book isn't just for your partner. This book is also for you as a father-to-be. As you prepare to become a father, you'll learn about the emotional and psychological changes you might experience and how you can bond with your baby even before they are born.

The practical steps to prepare for your baby's arrival will also be covered. You'll learn how to set up the nursery and prepare for the financial impact of having a baby.

I will also guide what to expect during labor and childbirth and advise you on supporting your partner in this amazing but challenging experience.

Becoming a father for the first time can be exciting and terrifying. But with the right information and support, you can make it through every step. This book should provide you with all the information and tools you need to make this a memorable time in your life and be the best dad you can be to your baby.

BECOMING A DAD

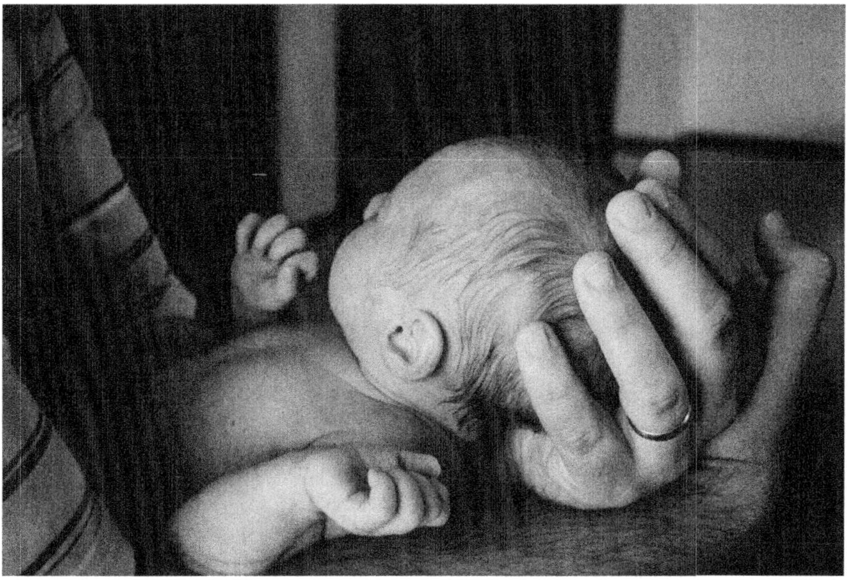

Being a father is an exciting and life-changing experience. It can be terrifying as well as exhilarating. The birth of a baby is an important milestone in your life, whether you are eagerly anticipating your first child's arrival or planning to add more children. This chapter will discuss what fatherhood is and how to prepare for this new adventure.

WHAT IS FATHERHOOD?

Fatherhood can be a complicated and multifaceted experience. It cannot be easy to understand. Fatherhood, at its core, is about building a meaningful and deep relationship with your child, helping them grow into happy, healthy, and well-adjusted adults.

Being present and involved in your child's life is one of the most important aspects of fatherhood. Being present and involved in your child's life means being there for them. Your role as a positive role model will include demonstrating kindness, empathy, and responsible behavior. You can encourage your child to be a positive role model and help them develop these qualities.

Fatherhood means taking care of your child, both emotionally and physically. This includes ensuring your child has adequate food, shelter, and medical care. This means that you must be sensitive to your child's emotions and provide a nurturing and safe environment for them to grow and thrive.

Helping your child develop self-worth and identity is another important aspect of fatherhood. It involves supporting your child in their passions and goals and encouraging them to have a positive self-image. You can help your child overcome life's difficulties by fostering self-esteem.

Fatherhood requires you to be a lifelong learner, adapting to your child's needs. Your role as a father will change and evolve as your child develops. Your role as a father will change over time. You must be sensitive to your child's interests and needs. Be open to changing your parenting style. You can create a lasting and loving relationship with your child by being open-minded and flexible.

Fatherhood can be a rewarding and multifaceted experience. It requires patience, dedication, willingness, and the ability to learn and grow. You can create a lasting and meaningful relationship with your child by being present, involved, and providing for their emotional and physical needs.

PREPARING FOR BIG CHANGES

Being a father means that there are many changes ahead. New responsibilities will be required, and you'll need to adjust to a new way of living. You can expect less sleep, more free time, and greater financial obligations. You should prepare mentally and emotionally for these changes and have the plan to help you adapt.

Being a father is not easy. You will experience significant changes when a baby arrives in your life. It is important to be prepared for these changes. These tips help you prepare for the changes that fatherhood brings.

Establish a support system: This is one of the most important things you can do to prepare for fatherhood. You might have other dads, friends, or family members who can provide emotional support and practical help when needed. For example, joining a group of new dads can help you connect with other fathers going through similar situations.

You need to know about infant care if you are a new dad. You will need to know how to change a diaper, burp, and soothe your baby when they are upset. To help you prepare for caring for newborns, it might be worth taking a parenting class and reading a book about infant care.

Be prepared for sleep deprivation. One of the most significant changes in fatherhood is sleep loss. You will likely be up several times a night to care for your baby. This can hurt your energy and general well-being. To prepare, you may want to adjust your sleeping schedule for the first few weeks before your baby arrives. Adjusting to a new sleeping schedule can be made easier by getting used to sleeping earlier or taking naps during the day.

A budget is important: The birth of a baby can cause significant financial changes. You should create a budget to cover the additional costs of formula and diapers. If you and your partner intend to return to work after the birth of your baby, you might need to account for child care costs. A budget can be a great way to prepare for fatherhood.

Talk about parenting styles with your partner: Before your baby arrives, it's important to discuss it with your partner. Talk about your parenting style, including how you will discipline your child and how you will handle disagreements. Also, discuss the values you wish to instill in your child. Talking openly about parenting can prepare you and your partner for this new stage in your life.

Preparing for major changes is a continuous process that requires patience, flexibility, and willingness to learn. You can be more confident and better equipped to care for your newborn by taking proactive steps to prepare. You'll be a better dad if you are kind to yourself and seek support when needed.

ORGANIZING PERSONAL LIFE

It's important to organize your life before your baby arrives. You must take care of all unfinished business, such as paying off your debts and repairing your home. It's also important to consider how you will manage your time once your baby arrives. You might consider creating a schedule to help you prioritize your new responsibilities and make time for your partner.

Preparing for fatherhood involves organizing your personal life. This involves taking a proactive approach in planning for and preparing for the major changes that will come with caring for a baby. These tips help you organize and prepare for your baby's arrival.

Prepare your home for baby: It's crucial to ensure that your baby is comfortable and safe as you prepare for their arrival. You might need to set up a nursery or babyproof in your home. Also, you may need to purchase necessary items like a car seat, stroller, and crib. You can feel more confident as a dad by creating a safe and comfortable environment.

You should plan for time off work. If you are going to be away from work following the birth of your baby, it is important to communicate with your employer. Talking about your plans for parental leaves, creating a plan to cover your work while you are away, and setting expectations regarding when you will return to work is one examples of what this might look like. You can reduce stress by planning and ensuring you have the time to bond with your baby.

Take care of yourself: It's crucial that you take care of your health as a dad so your baby can have the best possible start in life. It might mean getting enough sleep, exercising, and eating a healthy diet. You should also visit your doctor regularly, especially if there are underlying conditions.

Support system: It cannot be easy to care for a newborn. To help you get through the challenges, it is important to have a support network. You could join a dads' group or connect with other dads online. Or you might seek the support of your family and friends. A support system can make you more confident and ready to face this new stage in your life.

Self-care is a priority: It's easy for new dads to get overwhelmed by the demands of caring for and feeding a baby. It's crucial to remember to prioritize your self-care and to look after your mental and emotional well-being. You might find it helpful to relax, pursue hobbies that you love, or seek professional help if your anxiety or depression is severe.

Organization of your personal life requires patience, dedication, and the willingness to learn. You can feel more prepared and confident to face the joys and challenges of caring for a newborn by taking a proactive approach to planning and preparing. You'll be a better dad if you care for yourself, have a support network, and prioritize your health.

ORGANIZING YOUR PROFESSIONAL LIFE

You may need to adjust your work schedule to become a father. Your partner or baby may require you to take time off from work. You might also need to change your work schedule to meet your new responsibilities. Communicate with your employer to create a plan that will allow you to manage your family and work commitments.

Another important part of fatherhood preparation is organizing your professional life. These are additional tips to help you get organized for your baby's arrival and manage your professional responsibilities.

Communicate with your employer. It is important to discuss with your employer your plans for parental leave and any changes that might be required once your baby arrives. Your needs and expectations should be clear, and you can work with your employer on a plan that suits your needs.

It can be difficult to balance your professional responsibilities and the demands of caring for a newborn. A schedule with work and care for your baby is one way to stay organized. You might schedule work during nap time or work from home on some days.

Prioritize tasks: Being a dad is more difficult than ever. Prioritize your tasks and prioritize the most urgent and important tasks. This will allow you to be more productive and efficient in your professional life while still giving your baby the care they deserve.

Use technology: Technology can help new dads balance work and family responsibilities. Use tools such as video conferencing, instant messaging, email, or email to keep in touch with clients and colleagues even when you aren't at work.

Get support: If you are having trouble balancing your professional responsibilities and caring for a newborn child, don't hesitate to ask for help. Talk to your partner or other parents who have gone through similar situations, or seek professional counsel or counseling.

Organization of your professional life requires planning and communication. It also requires flexibility and adaptability. You can feel more confident and ready to tackle this new stage of your life by taking proactive steps toward organizing. You'll be a better dad at work and home if you prioritize your family.

BABYPROOFING YOUR HOME

Baby-proofing your home is one of the best things you can do in preparation for your newborn. You must take steps to make your home safe for your baby. This includes installing baby gates and securing electrical outlets. Also, make sure that hazardous substances and substances are out of reach. You also have a first-aid kit in case of an emergency.

Preparing for fatherhood is as important as baby-proofing your house. Babies love exploring their environment and can be very curious. This can lead to accidents and injuries. These tips help you baby-proof your house and provide a safe environment.

Begin by looking at your baby's eyes: This is one of the best ways to identify potential hazards in your house. This will allow you to see potential hazards from a different perspective and may help you spot them that you didn't know existed.

Secure electronics and furniture: Babies love pulling themselves up on furniture. This can prove dangerous for them. Bookcases, dressers, and other furniture should be securely attached to the wall. Cord covers are a good idea to keep wires and cord out of reach. Outlet covers will prevent your baby's fingers from getting into electrical outlets.

Certain hazardous items: Keep hazardous items, such as medications, cleaning supplies, and sharp objects, locked away and out of reach. You might consider installing childproof locks in drawers and cabinets to prevent your baby's access to potentially dangerous items.

Baby gates can be installed: Baby gates create a safe area for your child. Baby gates can be installed at the top and bottom stairs and indoors in rooms you don't want your baby to go.

Be sure to inspect your window treatments. Blinds and curtains can be strangulation hazards for babies. You can replace your window treatments with cordless ones or securely tie the strings and cords.

Avoid small objects: Children can choke on small objects like coins, batteries, or other small items. These items should be kept out of reach. You might also consider purchasing a small parts tester to check the size of small objects.

Baby-proofing your home is an important step toward fatherhood. You can feel more comfortable and confident as you go through the first stages of parenthood by taking proactive steps to ensure your baby is safe. As your baby grows, reviewing and improving your safety measures is important. Also, be sure to keep your baby safe.

Baby-proofing is a continuous process. You'll need to assess your home as your child grows and becomes more mobile. You can help your child explore the world by being proactive and vigilant.

Being a father is an amazing journey. It will bring you joy, challenges, and personal growth. You can be confident and prepared for the changes ahead by being aware of them. The fatherhood journey is never static, whether you are a new dad or an old one. It's always changing, and it's an honor to be part of it. Be present, supportive, open-minded, and available to your child, and you will be on your way to building a loving and strong relationship.

FACING THE FIRST TRIMESTER

As you prepare for the arrival of a new baby into the world, the first trimester is a thrilling time for you and your partner. It can also be a time when you must adjust to the first trimester's emotional and physical changes. This chapter will discuss the various aspects of the first trimester. We'll discuss medical exams, fetal growth, symptoms, and potential complications.

HAPPY ANNOUNCEMENT

The happy announcement is when expecting parents share their joy with family and friends. It is an emotional and exciting time. The way you announce your news will be very personal.

Some couples wait until the second trimester to share the news. This is because the chance of miscarriage being averted is lower. Some people prefer to tell their loved ones immediately, while others may wait until the end of the first trimester to share the news.

You can announce in person, by phone or video chat, or creatively via a post on social media or bespoke gifts. It doesn't matter what approach you choose; it is important to consider your loved ones' reactions and feelings.

Sometimes, loved ones might react differently to your expectations. Some people may feel overjoyed or excited, while others might have questions or concerns. It is important to be open to all possible reactions and to communicate honestly and openly with your closest friends and family.

This happy announcement can also be a chance to begin building a support network for the coming months. Friends and family can provide emotional and practical support throughout pregnancy. This could include listening to the baby, providing childcare assistance, and even helping with household chores.

The happy announcement is an important moment in the journey toward fatherhood. It's important that you approach it with consideration and thoughtfulness, as well as consider the needs and feelings of others around you.

COMMUNICATING IT WITH FRIENDS AND FAMILY

It can be exciting to share the news with your partner that you are expecting a child. However, it can also be nerve-wracking. Most couples wait until the second trimester to announce their pregnancy. This is because the chance of miscarriage drops dramatically. The decision about when and how to announce your pregnancy is personal and should be made according to your comfort level and circumstances.

You should consider some things when communicating your pregnancy to family and friends.

- Timing: Many couples wait until the last trimester of their first trimester to announce their baby's news. There is no wrong or right way to share the news. Remember that it is public once you share the news, which may draw much attention.
- Method: There are many options for sharing your pregnancy news. You can make a simple text message or phone call or post it on social media. You and your partner should decide what is most comfortable and authentic for them. Don't feel pressured or forced to do anything if it doesn't make you feel comfortable.

- Whom to tell: It is a good idea to share the news with your closest family and friends before you announce it to the world. This will allow you to feel more in control and let you share the news on your terms.
- Expect different reactions to the news of your pregnancy. Some people might be excited and overjoyed, while others might be more reserved or negative. Keep in mind that everyone is different and has different perspectives. Don't take negative reactions personally.

Communicating your pregnancy news can be both emotional and thrilling. Consider what is best for you and your partner. Don't be afraid to ask for help if needed.

FIRST MEDICAL EXAMINATION

It is important to schedule your first exam after you have found out that you are pregnant. Your doctor will perform a physical exam and check your weight and blood pressure. He or she may also ask about your medical history. A blood test may be performed to confirm pregnancy and determine if there are any other medical conditions.

It is crucial for both mother and baby to have the first medical exam during pregnancy. These are the things you can expect at these initial appointments.

1. Confirming pregnancy: This is the first step in prenatal care. This can be done by a blood or urine test to confirm the presence of the human chorionic hormone (hCG) after fertilization.
2. Health Assessment: After pregnancy has been confirmed, the mother's overall condition will be evaluated. This will include checking the mother's weight, blood pressure, medical history, and other pertinent information. It is crucial to tell your doctor about any medical conditions or medications you are taking.
3. Blood tests: A range of tests are performed to check for possible health problems. These tests may include testing for

HIV, blood type, Rh factor, anemia, and immunity to certain diseases.

4. Ultrasound: The ultrasound is done between weeks 8-12 to confirm the due date and check for the development of your fetus. The doctor can view the placenta, amniotic fluid, and fetus during an ultrasound. This will allow the doctor to determine if the pregnancy has developed normally and any possible complications.
5. Genetic Testing: This is the most common time genetic testing is offered, particularly if the mother is older than 35 years or has a history of genetic disorders. A nuchal translucency test measures the thickness of the skin at the back of the baby's neck and can be combined with a blood test to check for Down syndrome or other chromosomal abnormalities.
6. Education: The doctor can educate the mother and the father about what to expect during pregnancy at the first medical exam. They might discuss common pregnancy symptoms, prenatal vitamins, and healthy eating habits.

For a healthy pregnancy, it is important to attend all prenatal appointments. Prenatal care can help mothers increase their chances of a healthy pregnancy and delivery and detect and resolve any issues before they become serious.

FIRST ULTRASOUND SCAN

Your first ultrasound scan will be performed around the 8th week. The non-invasive ultrasound scan uses high-frequency sound waves to take images of your baby. It also helps your doctor track the development of your baby. Many expectant parents find the first ultrasound a wonderful moment. It is when they finally see their baby for the first time.

A first ultrasound scan, usually performed between weeks 8-12, is a significant milestone in the first trimester. Here are some things you can expect from an ultrasound scan.

Confirming pregnancy: The primary purpose of the first ultrasound to confirm that the pregnancy has been confirmed is to confirm a viable fetus in the uterus. An ultrasound will confirm a gestational sac and a fetal pod. These are signs that an embryo is developing.

Checking Fetal Development: An ultrasound technician will measure the fetus to establish the gestational date and confirm its age. The technician will measure the fetus' size, length, and head. A heartbeat is an indicator that the pregnancy is moving along well.

Assessment of Placenta & Amniotic Fluid: An ultrasound will check for the placenta's health and the amount of amniotic liquid surrounding the fetus. The function of the placenta, which provides oxygen and nutrients to the fetus, can impact the pregnancy's health. The amniotic liquid protects the fetus as well as helps regulate its temperature.

Identifying Multiples: A first ultrasound can also determine if more than one fetus is developing. This stage can identify twins, triplets, and more.

Reassurance: Many expectant parents find the first ultrasound an exciting and emotional moment. It provides the first visual confirmation that the developing fetus is real. This can reassure parents about the progress of their pregnancy and give a glimpse at the developing baby inside.

Although the first ultrasound is routine, expectant parents should attend the appointment. The doctor will recommend any follow-up actions. The doctor will discuss the next steps if abnormalities are detected during an ultrasound. These may include additional testing, monitoring, or intervention.

THE DEVELOPMENT OF THE FETUS DURING THE FIRST THREE MONTHS

Your baby's first trimester is a time of significant development. Their organs and bodies begin to form. Look at some of the most important milestones in fetal development over the first three months.

THE FIRST 6 WEEKS

Your baby is called an embryo during the first six weeks. The embryo is a small mass of cells that will eventually develop into a fully formed baby. The formation of the neural tube (which will eventually become the brain, spinal cord, and circulatory system) is one of the most important events during the first six weeks.

THE DEVELOPMENT FROM WEEK 7 TO WEEK 12.

Your baby enters the fetal phase of development between weeks 7-12. They grow quickly and take on more human-like features. They will start to respond to sound and touch and move and react to external stimuli. Your baby will have developed all major organs and systems by the end of the first trimester. However, there will still be a lot to learn.

FIRST TRIMESTER SYMPTOMS

Although fetal development is the main focus of the first trimester's attention, it is important not to overlook changes happening to your body. Many women feel a variety of emotional and physical symptoms during this period.

- Nausea and vomiting
- Fatigue
- Tenderness to the breast
- Mood swings
- Aversions to or cravings for food
- Frequent urination
- Constipation
- Headaches

These symptoms are normal during pregnancy. However, you must speak to your doctor if they become severe or disrupt your daily life.

Possible complications of the First Trimester

Although most pregnancies go smoothly, there can be complications in the first trimester. These complications include:

EARLY MISCARRIAGE IN PREGNANCY

Miscarriage can occur in the first trimester. Around 10-20% of miscarriages are reported. It can be heartbreaking for expectant parents. However, it is usually not caused by your or your partner's actions.

WHAT IS EXTRA URINE PREGNANCY?

An extra-uterine pregnancy (also known as an Ectopic pregnancy) is another potential problem. When the fertilized egg implants outside the uterus, most often in the fallopian tubes. Ectopic pregnancy is a medical emergency that requires immediate attention to avoid serious complications.

PREGNANCY TERMINATION

It is important to allow yourself to grieve after a miscarriage or any other termination of your pregnancy. You can also seek support from family members, friends, and professionals. You can also find resources to help you deal with the emotional and physical consequences of losing your baby.

FOODS TO AVOID WITH YOUR PARTNER DURING PREGNANCY

It is important to know what your partner eats during the first trimester. Some foods pose a risk for the developing fetus. It's important to limit or avoid certain foods.

- Raw and undercooked meats, poultry, and fish
- Unpasteurized dairy products
- Raw eggs and foods containing raw eggs
- Deli meats and other processed meats
- Mercury-rich fish include certain types

The first trimester can be an emotional rollercoaster with many physical and psychological changes. It is important to take care of yourself, communicate with your partner and medical professionals, and celebrate milestones in fetal development. You can ensure a happy and healthy pregnancy by being proactive and staying informed.

THE ARRIVAL OF THE SECOND TRIMESTER

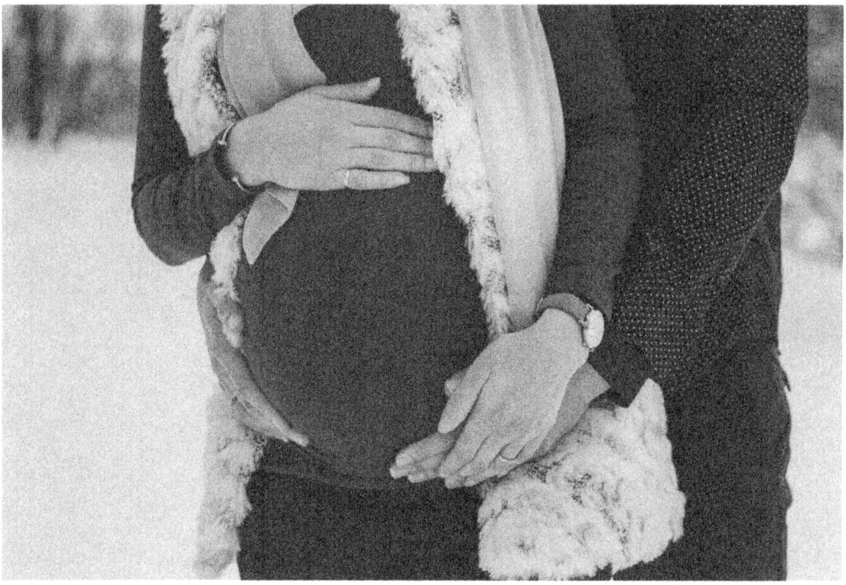

Congratulations, dad-to-be! Congratulations, dad-to-be! You have completed the first trimester. Now you are in the second trimester. This is a very exciting time for you both, as you will begin to notice major changes and milestones during pregnancy.

The second trimester usually begins on week 13 and ends on week 28. This is when the baby's growth rate accelerates, and the mother-to-be may feel more energetic and comfortable. These are just a few topics to remember as you move into the second trimester.

THE FOURTH & FIFTH MONTHS

The dad-to-be and the mom-to-be will find the fourth and fifth months of pregnancy exciting. The baby's development and growth continue at an incredible pace. Mom-to-be may feel the baby's first movements. These are the major developments and changes you can expect in the fourth and fifth trimesters of pregnancy.

1. Baby's growth: The baby grows to approximately 6 inches in length and 4 ounces in weight during the fourth month. The baby is approximately 10 inches in length by the end of the fifth and has nearly doubled its weight.
2. Facial Features: As the baby grows, the baby's facial features may begin to appear more like a newborn. The baby's eyes become closer together, his ears are in the final position, and his hair and nails begin to grow.
3. Movement: The mother-to-be might feel her baby's movements in the fourth and fifth months. These movements can feel like tiny kicks, bubbles, or flutters. Both parents can find this exciting and uplifting.
4. Weight Gain: As the baby grows and develops, the mom-to-be will likely gain weight in the fourth and fifth months. Your partner should be supported and encouraged to make healthy

decisions to ensure that the baby and she receives the nutrition they need.

5. Emotional changes: As she adjusts to pregnancy's physical and hormonal changes, the mom-to-be might experience some emotional changes in the fourth and fifth months. During this period, it is important to be understanding, patient, and supportive.
6. Prenatal Care: The mom-to-be will continue receiving regular prenatal care through her healthcare provider during the fourth and fifth months. These will include regular checkups to monitor the baby's growth and development, as well as check on the health of the mother-to-be.

The fourth and fifth trimesters of pregnancy may bring on some physical changes, including:

1. An increase in appetite: The baby's growth may cause the mother-to-be to feel more hungry and require her to eat more often.
2. Fatigue: Mom-to-be might feel fatigued during the fourth and fifth months, but she may feel more energetic as the pregnancy progresses.
3. Back Pain: The baby may feel discomfort or pain as she grows and her body changes.

4. Braxton Hicks Contractions (Bristachio Hicks): These are mild contractions that can occur in the fourth or fifth month as the body prepares to give birth.
   The dad-to-be can become more involved in prenatal care as the second trimester progresses. It is good to start thinking about how to attend prepartum classes and help prepare for the baby's arrival. Prepartum classes are a great way to get valuable information and support in the final trimester.

THE SIXTH MONTH

Many expectant parents consider the sixth month of pregnancy a milestone. It marks the halfway point in a woman's pregnancy. It can be difficult for her as she might experience more discomfort or limitations.

The baby continues to develop and grow rapidly during the sixth month. They will measure between 11-14 inches in length and weigh about 1-2 pounds. They will develop more fat layers, regulating their body temperature and providing energy to grow. They will also develop their digestive and respiratory systems. They will be able to make breathing movements and swallow the amniotic liquid.

The sixth month can present new challenges for the mother-to-be. Growing a baby can cause pain and discomfort in the mother-to-be, including backaches, pelvic pain, and shortness of breathe. Her baby may experience swelling in her hands or feet, stretch marks, skin changes, and other symptoms.

Your partner should be supported during this time. Help her to find healthy and comfortable ways to live with you. Encourage your partner to get enough sleep, stay hydrated, and eat a healthy diet. Light exercises such as swimming or prenatal yoga can be beneficial to her. This can ease discomfort and promote relaxation.

Your partner may experience some emotional changes during the sixth month. As the reality of parenthood begins to sink in, your partner may feel anxious or overwhelmed. You can be supportive, understanding, and patient with your partner during this difficult time. Encourage her to discuss her feelings openly.

The sixth month of pregnancy can be challenging and exciting for expectant parents. You can make your partner feel more confident and comfortable as she enters the final months of her pregnancy by informing you about any developments and supporting your partner.

WHAT HAPPENS TO THE MOM-TO-BE?

The second trimester is when the baby grows and develops, and the mother-to-be experiences many emotional and physical changes. These are the most common changes that you will see in your partner during this period:

Weight Gain Weight gain can be a natural and healthy part of pregnancy. It's important that you support your partner in her adjustment to her new body. Women usually gain between 1-2 and 14 pounds during the second trimester.

Skin changes During pregnancy, many women experience skin changes, such as stretch marks, darkening of the skin (such as around the nipples or on the face), and acne. Your partner should feel confident and comfortable with her changing skin.

Mood swings During pregnancy, hormonal changes can lead to mood swings. You may notice your partner becoming more anxious, irritable, or weepy than usual. It's important to be understanding and patient during these times.

Fatigue Despite being called the "honeymoon" phase of pregnancy, many women still feel fatigued during the second trimester. To help ease the burden, encourage your partner to relax and ask for help with chores or other household duties.

Braxton Hicks Contractions - Your partner might experience Braxton Hicks contractions in the second trimester. These are contractions that prepare the uterus to go into labor. These contractions are usually normal and painless. However, if you feel uncomfortable or they become more frequent, talk to your doctor.

Backaches Your partner may experience back pain as her center of gravity shifts with your baby's growth. This can put a strain on her spine and back. To ease her back pain, offer to massage her back and encourage her to exercise and have good posture.

Your partner might feel short of breath as the baby grows and takes up more space within the uterus. Encourage your partner to take deep, slow breaths and refrain from doing anything that makes her feel tired or winded.

You can support your partner by understanding and supporting her through these changes. This will help her feel more confident and comfortable as she navigates pregnancy.

SECOND TRIMESTER EXAMINATIONS

Your partner will be subject to several medical exams during the second trimester. These examinations are necessary to monitor the baby's health and development. These exams must ensure your pregnancy is going as planned and identify possible complications. These are the most common second-trimester examinations you can expect.

Ultrasound Scans: Ultrasounds can be used to see the baby's development and detect any possible abnormalities. Your partner will typically have at least one ultrasound scan in the second trimester (weeks 18-22).

Blood tests: Your partner will be subject to several blood tests in the second trimester. These tests are done to determine if there are any complications, such as iron deficiency or gestational diabetes. These tests can also determine your partner's Rh factor and screen for infectious diseases that may affect the baby.

Glucose tolerance test: This screening tool is for gestational diabetics, a condition that can occur during pregnancy. To determine how well your body processes sugar, your partner must drink a sugary beverage.

Non-Stress Test - The non-stress testing is a non-invasive and simple test that evaluates the baby's well-being and health. The fetal monitor measures the baby's heartbeat and movements for approximately 20-30 minutes.

Anatomy scan: This ultrasound scan examines the baby's development and growth, including its limbs and bones. It can detect any potential complications or abnormalities.

Your partner's doctor will recommend that you attend all scheduled appointments. Early detection of potential problems can help to improve your chances of having a healthy baby and pregnancy. These examinations can also help you and your partner bond with your baby and make it easier to feel connected to the entire pregnancy experience.

UNDERSTANDING BLOOD TESTS

Prenatal care includes blood tests. They can give important information about the health and development of the mother and fetus. Blood tests are usually performed in the second trimester to check for possible complications and ensure the pregnancy moves as it should.

These are common blood tests that can be done during the second trimester.

1. Complete Blood Count (CBC). A complete blood count measures the number of different blood cells in the body. This test is useful in diagnosing anemia, infections, or other health issues.
2. The Rh Factor and Blood Type: Blood type and Rh factor are vital information during pregnancy. They can have a significant impact on the health of the baby. Rh incompatibility is when the mother is Rh negative and the baby Rh positive. This can lead to serious health problems for the baby.
3. Antibody Screen: An antibody screen is a test to check the mother's blood for antibodies that could attack the fetus. This may occur if the mother's type of blood is not compatible with that of the baby or if she has been exposed to certain infections.

4. Glucose tolerance test: A glucose tolerance test checks for gestational diabetics, a condition that can occur during pregnancy. This test requires that you drink a sugary beverage and have your blood drawn to determine blood sugar levels.
5. Hepatitis B surface antigen: The test detects the presence of the hepatitis B viral infection. This virus can be passed from mother to child during childbirth. The mother can stop transmission to her baby if she tests positive.

It is important to fully understand the purpose of each test and how they are conducted. Any abnormalities found may require further testing. Your partner's healthcare provider can help you develop a plan to manage any health problems.

Prenatal care is crucial for a healthy pregnancy and a healthy baby. Follow your partner's healthcare provider's instructions for monitoring her health and the baby's development.

OTHER TESTS DURING THE SECOND TRIMESTER

Your partner's doctor may recommend several tests during the second trimester to assess for possible health issues for her and the baby. These tests can detect potential problems early and enable timely interventions to ensure a healthy baby.

These are just a few tests that can be done during the second trimester.

1. Glucose tolerance test (GTT): The GTT is a blood test to check for gestational diabetes. This is a form of diabetes that occurs during pregnancy. If left untreated, it is a common condition that can cause serious health problems for both mother and baby. This involves drinking sugary solutions and having blood drawn to test blood sugar levels.
2. Group B Streptococcus Test GBS: (GBS) is a type of bacteria commonly found in both the genital tract and intestinal tracts of men and women. Although it is usually harmless, it can cause serious complications for newborns during birth. To check for GBS, the test involves swabbing your rectum and vagina.
3. Alpha-Fetoprotein Test: (AFP) This blood test checks for AFP levels in the mother's blood. AFP is a protein produced by the

developing fetus. A high level of AFP in the mother's body can indicate possible problems like neural tube defects and Down syndrome.

4. Non-Invasive Prenatal Testing (NIPT): NIPT is a blood test that can detect genetic abnormalities like Down syndrome and other chromosomal abnormalities. This involves analyzing the baby's DNA in the mother's blood.
5. Ultrasound of Fetus: An ultrasound is non-invasive and uses sound waves to create images. This test can be used to monitor the baby's growth and development and detect potential problems like structural abnormalities or low levels of amniotic fluid.

These tests are useful in identifying potential problems but are unnecessary for every pregnancy. Based on your partner's medical history and individual health, the doctor will recommend which tests to perform. To ensure you are informed and capable of making informed decisions regarding your partner's health, it is important that you discuss any concerns with her doctor.

SEX DURING PREGNANCY

It is an integral part of any relationship. During pregnancy, it can be a great way for couples to stay in touch and intimate. Many couples are unsure if it is safe to have sexual activity during pregnancy. They also wonder what precautions they should take to protect the baby and mother.

It is generally safe to have sex during pregnancy, especially in the second trimester. It is important to talk with your partner's healthcare provider if you have any questions or concerns. They can offer guidance and recommendations based on your partner's medical history and individual pregnancy.

These are some important things to remember about sex during pregnancy.

- Communication is important: Both partners must openly and honestly discuss their concerns and feelings regarding sex during pregnancy. You may feel uncomfortable, have hormonal fluctuations, or experience emotional changes that could affect your partner's desire to be sexually active. Talk to her healthcare provider about any concerns.

- Secure positions: Certain positions can be more comfortable as the pregnancy progresses. Avoid positions that place pressure on the abdomen, or cause pain or discomfort. To find comfortable and safe positions, consult your partner's healthcare provider.
- Take care: As pregnancy progresses, your cervix can become more sensitive and softer, increasing the chance of infection. Avoid activities that can cause injury or trauma to the cervix, such as vigorous or rough sex.
- Protect your baby: The amniotic fluid protects and seals the cervix. In general, sex is safe for the baby and does not cause premature labor. It is important to be gentle, cautious, and careful.
- Some women may feel less sexual desire when pregnant due to hormonal changes, fatigue, and other factors. This is normal and may vary from one woman to the next. Partners should be supportive and patient and openly discuss sexual desires or concerns.
- Some women may feel discomfort or pain while having sex. This could be due to medical conditions or physical changes. You must discuss your concerns with your

partner's healthcare provider. They can offer guidance and suggestions for managing the discomfort.

Communication, safety, and comfort are the most important aspects of sex during pregnancy. You can have a fulfilling and healthy sex life by working as a couple in this exciting, transformative time.

PREPARTUM CLASSES

Prepartum classes can help you prepare for your baby's arrival. These classes will teach your partner and you important skills about childbirth and breastfeeding.

The second trimester of pregnancy is a transformative and exciting time. You'll be ready to welcome your baby into the world by supporting your partner and keeping up-to-date with the latest developments and changes.

JUMPING INTO THE THIRD TRIMESTER

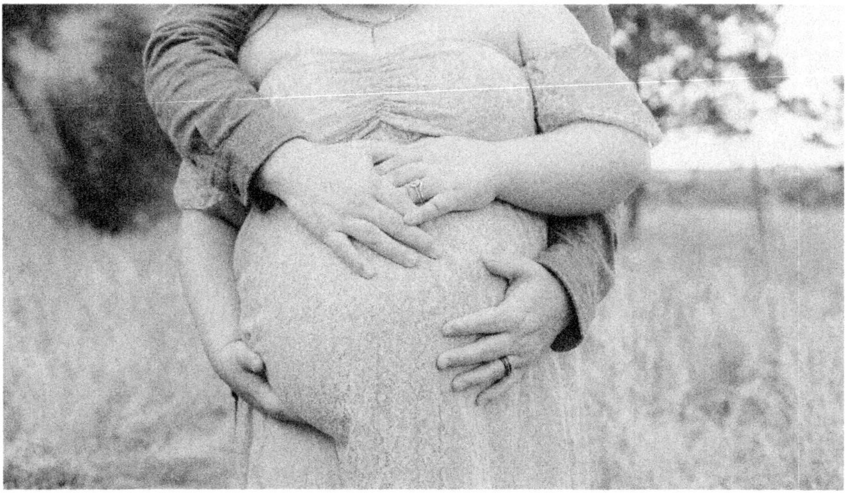

Expectant fathers will find the third trimester challenging and exciting. You may feel various emotions as your partner approaches their due date, including joy, anxiety, and nervousness. This chapter will cover what to expect in the final two months of pregnancy, signs you should be aware of, emotional changes, how to prepare for parenthood, and how to handle overwhelming family members.

THE BABY IS ALMOST READY

The third trimester, which is close to the due date, is crucial for the baby's growth. The baby is now ready to give birth and has developed all of their major organs.

The baby's brain will grow rapidly in the last weeks of pregnancy. They will continue to gain weight and develop their lungs, digestive system, and other organs. As they adjust and move in preparation for giving birth, the baby will become more active.

The baby should be fully developed by the end of the third trimester and ready to go outside the womb. It's important to remember that not all babies arrive at the exact same time; some may arrive sooner or later than others. It's crucial to prepare for the possibility that your baby will arrive early or late and to be flexible to change.

It is a good idea to keep in touch with your partner and their healthcare provider throughout the third trimester. This will ensure that you are prepared for any changes and developments. You can support your partner by staying involved and informed throughout the pregnancy. This will help you prepare for your exciting new baby's arrival.

THE LAST TWO MONTHS

The baby's rapid growth and development, and the mother might experience some emotional and physical changes during the last two months. These are some of the possible things that you can expect in this period:

1. Physical changes: As your baby grows, so will your partner's body. She might experience more fatigue, sleep problems, and frequent urination. She might also experience discomfort or back pain, as she may have difficulty finding a comfortable place to sit or lie down.
2. Braxton Hicks cramps: Braxton Hicks are mild contractions that prepare the uterus to go into labor. These contractions may feel like tightening the abdominal muscles or squeezing, but they are rarely painful.
3. Preparation for labor, delivery, and birth: Your partner might start to think about labor and delivery as the due date nears. You may find that your partner is interested in classes on childbirth or breastfeeding. She might also start to consider a birth plan. It is important to support and be involved in these preparations and to talk about any preferences or concerns your partner might have.

4. Emotional changes: As your partner prepares to welcome the baby, the last two months can be a time when you may experience emotional changes. You may notice that she may be anxious, overwhelmed, or experiencing mood swings and other emotional changes as she prepares to become a parent. It is important to be supportive and understanding and openly discuss any fears or concerns.

The last two months of pregnancy can be challenging and exciting as you prepare to welcome your baby. You can ensure a positive and healthy pregnancy by being attentive to your partner and working together.

SIGNS TO WATCH OUT FOR

Pay attention to any symptoms or signs that may indicate a problem during the third trimester. These are signs to look out for:

1. Contractions: Preterm labor can signify contractions, which can be very dangerous for the baby and the mom. Contact your healthcare provider immediately if your partner experiences painful and regular contractions.
2. Vaginal bleeding should be reported to your healthcare provider if you experience any vaginal bleeding while pregnant. This could be a sign that there is a serious problem, such as placenta previa.
3. Persistent or severe headaches: Although headaches are common in pregnancy, they can also be a sign that there is something wrong. Preeclampsia can cause severe headaches and high blood pressure, resulting in other health issues for both mother and baby.
4. Reduced fetal movements: It's normal for the baby to grow and run out of space, so it's not surprising that fetal movements may decrease. If your partner notices a decrease in movement, they should contact their healthcare provider.

5. Preterm labor can cause cramping or pain in the lower back or abdomen.
6. Preeclampsia can lead to swelling of the face, hands, or feet.
7. Vision changes: Preeclampsia can lead to blurred vision or other vision problems.

   It is important that your partner immediately seeks medical attention if they experience any of these symptoms. Sometimes, it is crucial to get medical attention immediately for the mother's health and the baby's safety.

EMOTIONAL CHANGES

Your partner might experience anxiety, fear, excitement, and a variety of other emotions during the third trimester. Feeling anxious and nervous about the future is normal as you get closer to your due date.

The following are some common emotions that women experience in the third trimester:

1. Anxiety: Your partner might feel anxious as the due date nears. She might worry about her ability to cope with the new challenges or the safety and health of the baby.
2. Excited: Many women feel excited as they end their pregnancies. As you prepare for your baby's arrival, this can be a time to celebrate joy and celebration.
3. Mood swings during pregnancy: Mood swings can occur due to hormonal changes. This can be particularly evident during the third trimester. You may notice sudden mood changes in your partner, including laughter or tears.
4. Fatigue: Your partner might feel tired as your baby grows and develops. This can lead to emotional overwhelm, making it more difficult to deal with the challenges of pregnancy.

It is important that you are supportive and understanding of the emotional changes experienced by a pregnant woman. You can listen patiently, offer reassurance and encouragement, or just be there when she needs you. You can work together to help each other through the third trimester's ups and downs and be ready for the exciting journey ahead by working as a team.

COUVADE DADS-TO BE

Couvade Syndrome is also known as "pregnancy symptoms for men" or "sympathetic pregnancy." It's a condition in which expectant fathers experience the same physical and emotional symptoms as their partners during pregnancy. These symptoms can include nausea, vomiting, mood swings, weight gain, and contractions.

Although the exact cause of Couvade syndrome is unknown, it is thought to be due to hormonal changes, stress, and emotional attachment to the child. According to some studies, fathers could use the symptoms to bond with their partners and prepare for fatherhood.

Couvade Syndrome symptoms can be discussed with your partner or healthcare provider if you have them. They can offer support and advice regarding managing your symptoms and dealing with emotional changes.

Couvade Syndrome, while a real condition that exists, is not recognized by medical professionals. Some healthcare providers may misunderstand or dismiss it. It can be a healthy and normal way for fathers and partners to communicate and plan for their baby's arrival.

EMPATHIZING WITH YOUR PARTNER

It is important to feel empathy with your partner during pregnancy. This will help maintain a supportive and healthy relationship. It can be difficult for your partner to cope with pregnancy.

Try empathizing and relating to your partner by putting yourself in their shoes. Listen to your partner when they share their concerns, fears, and emotions. Don't dismiss or minimize them.

You can also be proactive and offer support by helping with chores and running errands. It can show your partner you care and that you are invested in their wellbeing by taking the initiative to help them.

If your partner experiences mood swings or other emotional changes, it is important to be understanding and patient. Even the most patient person can feel overwhelmed or irritable from hormonal fluctuations and pregnancy stress. Keep calm, be supportive of their feelings, and not take their moods personally.

You can create a supportive and strong relationship with your partner by empathizing and understanding during pregnancy and beyond.

PREPARING TO PARENTHOOD

The third trimester is all about preparing for parenthood. These are some tips to help get you started:

1. You can take a parenting class: Many community centers and hospitals offer classes to help you and your partner prepare to welcome your baby. These classes include safety, infant care, breastfeeding, and safety.
2. Make a birth plan. A birth plan is a document that describes your preferences for labor and birth, pain management, and the delivery position. A birth plan will help you and your partner feel more in charge and better prepared for the birth.
3. You will need to set up your nursery as you approach the last weeks of pregnancy. You will need a crib, changing table, and a car seat. You should ensure that you only purchase safe, high-quality items and adhere to all safety guidelines.
4. Self-care is important: Parenthood can be overwhelming and stressful. It's also important to take care of your partner and yourself. It includes healthy eating, exercising, sleeping, and

managing stress. Spend time doing things you love, like reading, walking, and spending time with friends.

5. Talk to other parents. Talking with other parents can provide valuable advice and support. To share your stories and learn from others, reach out to family members, friends, or online communities.

These steps will help you ensure a positive transition to parenthood and allow you to enjoy this transformative time in life.

OVERCOMING FEAR OF NOT BEING GOOD ENOUGH

Expectant fathers often feel anxious or afraid about being a good parents as the due date nears. For first-time fathers, this can be particularly true.

It's okay to feel like this. You can do many things to overcome self-doubt, prepare for parenthood, and get over your fears.

Education about your baby's first few months and weeks is important. Talk to other parents, take classes, read articles and books, and get an idea of what to expect.

It is important to take care of your mental and emotional well-being. You should make time for yourself, such as meditation, exercise, and hobbies you enjoy. If you are struggling, seek support from family members, friends, and therapists.

Remember that not everyone is perfect and that mistakes are normal. It is important to communicate openly with your partner and to work as a team to face the challenges of parenthood.

Keep your eyes open and positive, and remember to enjoy the excitement of helping a new life enter the world. You can overcome your fears with patience, dedication, and the willingness to learn and grow. Your child will be a loving and supportive parent.

DEALING WITH OVERWHELMING FAMILY MEMBERS

It can be difficult to deal with overwhelmed family members at any stage of pregnancy. However, it can be especially challenging in the third trimester, when emotions and tensions can be high. These are some ways to navigate this situation.

1. Establish boundaries: It is important to establish clear boundaries with family members that may be too demanding or overwhelming. You could limit your time with them or set ground rules for communication or visits.
2. Open communication: Communicate honestly and openly with your family about your expectations and needs. If you feel overwhelmed or stressed, let them know, and they will be able to help. Try to be firm and kind, and find a compromise that works well for everyone.
3. Ask for support from your partner. Your partner can be an excellent source of support when dealing with overwhelmed family members. Talk to your partner about your concerns, and we can find solutions together.

4. Get outside help: A counselor or therapist may be able to offer support if you are having trouble coping with overwhelming family members. These professionals can help you to develop coping strategies and set boundaries. They can also help you work through any emotions or difficulties that may arise.

   Your health and that of your baby should always come first. To ensure a healthy and safe pregnancy, don't be afraid of prioritizing your needs and setting boundaries when necessary.

BE PREPARED FOR ANYTHING

It is an amazing journey that marks the beginning of a new chapter in a couple's lives. Although it is a time of excitement, joy, and anticipation, it can also bring anxiety, fear, or complications. Every pregnancy is different, and there are many ways to prepare for the unexpected. However, it is important to be prepared and well-informed to deal with any situation.

Complications can occur at any stage of pregnancy. Be prepared. There are many medical conditions that a pregnant woman can experience that can have a significant impact on her health and the health of her baby, including preeclampsia and gestational diabetes. These conditions can be serious, so it is important to know what to look for.

The mother-to-be and her partner can experience anxiety and stress from pregnancy complications. It is important to stay calm, be positive, and communicate with your healthcare provider to make informed decisions about the health of the mother and baby. You should also keep up to date with the most recent research and advances in prenatal care. This will help you make the best decisions possible for your family.

Being prepared for anything can also mean being able to deal with any psychological or emotional challenges that may occur during pregnancy. Hormonal fluctuations in pregnancy, such as anxiety, mood swings, and depression, can cause various emotions. These emotions should be acknowledged and addressed. You can also seek help from your family members, partner, and healthcare provider.

Being prepared for any situation during pregnancy is about being proactive, knowledgeable, and adaptable. It is important to know the signs and symptoms of possible complications, what to expect at each stage, and to have a plan for dealing with any eventuality. Although pregnancy can be unpredictable, staying informed and having a support team is possible.

MEDICAL COMPLICATIONS

It is crucial to keep track of your health during pregnancy and that of your growing baby. Expectant parents can be worried and stressed by medical complications. Hypertension, diabetes, placenta previa, and hypertension are just a few medical problems that can arise during pregnancy.

If left untreated, hypertension (also known as high blood pressure) can cause serious complications for the baby and mother. Pre-eclampsia can be a serious condition that can lead to death. It is characterized by high blood sugar and organ damage, such as the liver and kidneys. It is important to consult your healthcare provider about managing hypertension during pregnancy. Follow their recommendations regarding medications, lifestyle modifications, monitoring, and other measures.

Both type 1 and 2 diabetes can complicate pregnancy. High blood sugar levels can harm the developing fetus and cause congenital disabilities, premature deliveries, and other complications. A healthcare provider must be able to monitor and manage women who have had diabetes before pregnancy or develop gestational diabetes during pregnancy. Treatments may include insulin injections, diet changes, and regular monitoring of blood sugar levels.

Placenta previa refers to a condition where the placenta completely covers the cervix. Vaginal bleeding can occur, putting both mother and baby at high risk during birth. To reduce bleeding, women with placenta Previa should consider having a Cesarean Section.

Medical complications during pregnancy are not the mother's or father-to-be's responsibility. To ensure the best outcome for the mother and baby, it is important to remain positive, follow all medical advice, and work with healthcare professionals. Many pregnancies affected by medical problems can be saved with proper care and attention.

ABSOLUTE REST

Absolute rest is a recommendation from a doctor for women with complications during pregnancy, such as high blood pressure and placenta previa. Absolute rest is when a woman must stay in bed for most of the day. She should avoid physical exertion and keep her feet off the ground as much as possible.

As a preventative measure, absolute rest is often recommended to lower the chance of premature labor or preterm birth. Women who have been used to being independent and active may find it difficult to adjust to this situation. To avoid any complications, it is important that you follow the recommendations to ensure the best outcome for your baby and mother.

Women with children or work obligations may find absolute rest difficult. Talking with your healthcare provider can help you devise a plan for managing these responsibilities and prioritizing rest.

Women on absolute rest should not only stay in bed but also limit their physical activity and avoid any positions that may put extra pressure on the uterus. This could include not lifting heavy objects or standing for long periods.

Women on absolute rest should be able to maintain their mental and emotional health. It is possible to keep in touch with family and friends, pursue hobbies and interests, and seek professional support.

Following the advice for absolute rest is crucial in managing pregnancy complications and ensuring the best outcome for the mother and baby. It cannot be easy to adapt to a more sedentary lifestyle. However, it is important to prioritize rest and follow all medical advice to avoid further complications.

ABNORMALITIES IN ULTRASOUND

Ultrasound is an important tool in prenatal care that monitors the development and growth of the fetus. Although it is most commonly used to detect potential problems early in pregnancy, ultrasound abnormalities can also be detected later. Ultrasound abnormalities may vary in severity and indicate various problems, such as genetic conditions or developmental delays.

Ultrasound may detect structural abnormalities in the brain, heart, kidneys, and limbs. While some structural abnormalities are insignificant and do not require treatment, others can be more serious and require medical attention.

Ultrasound can sometimes be used to detect genetic conditions. These include chromosomal abnormalities, such as Down syndrome. They can be detected using a combination of blood tests and ultrasound imaging. Some genetic conditions are not likely to impact the baby's quality of life or health, but others could require ongoing medical care and early intervention.

Ultrasound can also detect developmental delays, such as slow growth and poor blood flow to the placenta. These delays could be due to several factors, including gestational diabetes, hypertension, or other medical conditions. Medical interventions may be required to avoid further complications if they are identified.

Not all abnormalities found by ultrasound should be considered alarming. It is important to discuss any abnormalities with your healthcare provider. They can help you understand your baby's development and health implications. Sometimes additional monitoring or testing may be required. Your healthcare provider will help you to understand what to expect and how to prepare.

It is important to be informed about your prenatal care and regular ultrasounds. You can prepare for any problems by understanding the risks and knowing what to expect.

DEFECTS IN THE FETUS

Expectant parents should be concerned about the possibility of fetal defects or abnormalities. Fetal abnormalities can be structural or functional defects that affect the development and health of the fetus. These defects can also be detected during prenatal screening, ultrasound scans, and genetic testing.

Many factors can lead to fetal abnormalities, including genetic mutations, environmental factors, and complications that may have occurred during pregnancy. Congenital heart and neural tube defects are some of the most common fetal abnormalities. Expectant parents can find it difficult to accept a diagnosis of a fetal anomaly. It is important to seek guidance and emotional support from your healthcare provider during this difficult time.

The severity and type of fetal abnormalities will determine the treatment options. Some conditions require immediate medical attention after birth. Others may require ongoing medical treatment and surgeries. Sometimes, medical intervention is not possible, and parents might need to plan for the termination of the pregnancy.

While a diagnosis of a fetal anomaly can be very devastating, it doesn't necessarily mean that the baby won't live a happy and fulfilled life. With the right support and care, many children with fetal anomalies become successful and healthy adults.

Expectant parents can feel anxious and stressed about the possibility of fetal abnormalities. It's important to be informed about prenatal screenings, to seek medical attention, and to have a support system to help you navigate any difficulties that might arise. Families can overcome any obstacle to ensure their child has the best possible start in life with the right support and care.

FETAL DEATH

Fetal death is also known as a stillbirth. It occurs when a baby's body dies after only 20 weeks of gestation. It is a devastating experience for both parents that can cause grief, stress, and pain. Understanding the risk factors and causes of fetal death and signs and symptoms can help you recognize a problem.

Several factors, including maternal age and smoking, drug and alcohol abuse, preexisting medical conditions, and genetic abnormalities, can increase the risk of fetal deaths. Sometimes, the cause of fetal deaths cannot be determined. In other cases, however, complications or medical conditions may be involved.

A sudden decrease in fetal movement or vaginal bleeding can be signs of fetal death. It is important to remember that symptoms accompany not all cases. Sometimes, women don't realize their baby is dead until they have an ultrasound or another medical examination.

Your healthcare provider may perform tests to confirm fetal death if it is suspected. An ultrasound or non-stress test may evaluate the baby's heartbeat and movements. There may be several options depending on the circumstances and time of the fetal deaths. Some cases may allow labor to be induced, while others may require a cesarean.

It can be extremely difficult to deal with the death of a baby. It takes time to grieve and heal. There is no right or wrong way. Many mothers find comfort in talking with a psychiatrist or joining a support group for parents who have lost their children. Having a support partner, family member, and healthcare provider can offer emotional support and guidance during these difficult times is important.

Fetal death can be a very serious event. It is important to take every precaution to avoid this. A healthy lifestyle, regular prenatal visits, and monitoring fetal movements are all steps that can be taken to ensure a healthy pregnancy. It is important to seek guidance and support during fetal loss. This will help you to deal with the grief and move on.

PREMATURE DELIVERY

Premature birth is a serious, often unanticipated problem that can arise during pregnancy. Premature delivery refers to the birth of a baby before the 37th week. Many factors can lead to premature delivery, including infection, placental complications, and abnormalities. Sometimes, it is impossible to determine the exact cause of premature birth.

Both the baby and the mother can be at risk from premature delivery. Premature delivery can increase the chances of developing health issues such as cerebral palsy, respiratory distress syndrome, vision and hearing problems, and developmental delays. These health problems can be severe or mild and can have long-lasting consequences.

Premature delivery can cause emotional and physical distress for the mother. Premature delivery can increase your risk of depression after birth, as well as complications like bleeding, infection, and difficulty breastfeeding.

Getting medical attention as soon as a woman experiences premature labor is important. To delay delivery, the healthcare provider might use tocolytic drugs, magnesium sulfate, or corticosteroids to speed up the baby's growth. Sometimes, it is necessary to deliver the baby early to preserve the health of the mother and the baby.

Women can take steps to decrease their chance of having a premature birth. These include seeking prenatal care early, avoiding drug and alcohol abuse, and managing chronic conditions like high blood pressure and diabetes.

Even with the best medical and preventive care, premature delivery can still happen. It is important to prepare for this possibility and seek support from family members, friends, and healthcare providers during difficult times. The mother and baby can recover from premature births if they receive the right care and support.

RECOGNIZING THE RISKS

Recognizing and addressing the risks of pregnancy is an important step to ensure the safety and health of the baby and mother. Many complications can occur during pregnancy. Some may prove to be life-threatening.

High blood pressure, gestational diabetic, preterm labor, and placenta previa are some of the most prevalent risks in pregnancy. Regular prenatal checks and tests can help identify these risks and monitor them. Additional factors that can increase your risk of complications in pregnancy include smoking, excess weight, and previous complications.

These are the most common risks. However, there are other, less serious, but still very real risks, such as preeclampsia and eclampsia. These conditions need immediate medical attention. If left untreated, they can lead to stillbirth or premature birth.

Women must be aware of potential risks and report any concerns to their healthcare provider immediately. Vaginal bleeding, severe headaches, and vision changes are all signs of a problem.

Not all risks can be prevented or identified, even with prenatal care. In the event of an emergency, it is important to have a plan. This includes knowing the exact location of emergency services or hospitals and having a support system.

Recognizing and dealing with pregnancy risks is essential to ensure the safety and health of the baby and mother. Women can manage their risks by working with a healthcare provider, being aware of possible symptoms, and taking proactive steps to ensure a healthy pregnancy.

DEALING WITH GUILT

While pregnancy is an exciting time full of anticipation and joy, it can also bring about stress, worry, and guilt. Expectant mothers can feel guilty for many reasons. These include not eating right, not exercising enough, and not being prepared for their baby's arrival. Fathers-to-be may feel guilty for not being able or willing to help more during pregnancy.

Guilt is a difficult emotion to manage, especially when you are pregnant. It is important to recognize that guilt can be normal and manageable. Here are some ways to deal with guilt during pregnancy.

1. Be kind to yourself. Recognize that everyone is imperfect and that mistakes are bound to happen. Forgive yourself for your perceived mistakes, and be kind to yourself.
2. Talk to your partner. You may find support and perspective from them.
3. Get professional help: Don't be ashamed to seek professional assistance if you are struggling with guilt or other emotional issues. Counselors or therapists can offer support and strategies to manage your emotions.

4. Concentrate on the positive. Instead of dwelling on what isn't working, focus on what is. Recognize your achievements and successes.
5. Keep informed. Learn as much information as possible about pregnancy and childbirth to feel confident and empowered in your choices.

Guilt is a normal and healthy emotion. However, it does not have to be controlling your pregnancy experience. You can control your emotions and have a wonderful time during this special time of your life with the right strategies and support.

COMMON PROBLEMS

While pregnancy is healthy and natural, it can bring about some problems. These problems can be severe and affect a woman's pregnancy quality. These are the top problems women face during pregnancy.

Nausea, vomiting, and nausea: These symptoms are most common during the first trimester. Although it is commonly called "morning nausea," it can also occur at any hour of the day. Women can experience nausea and vomiting, which can be severe or mild.

1. Fatigue: Fatigue can occur in the first trimester. It is usually caused by hormonal changes or the body's increased energy needs. Fatigue can be relieved by proper nutrition and rest.
2. Back pain: Pregnancy can cause back pain. It is usually caused by the baby's weight and the changes in the mother's center of gravity. Back pain can be relieved by gentle exercise, good posture, and supportive shoes.
3. Heartburn: This is caused by hormonal changes that relax the digestive tract muscles. Heartburn can be relieved by eating smaller meals and avoiding acidic and spicy foods.
4. Swelling: In the latter stages of pregnancy, swelling is more common, particularly in the ankles and feet. The body retains

extra fluids to help the baby grow. Swelling can be reduced by drinking plenty of fluids, elevating your legs, and wearing supportive shoes.

5. Constipation: This is caused by hormonal changes and the pressure placed on the digestive tract by the growing uterus. Constipation can be reduced by eating a high-fiber diet, drinking lots of water, and being active.
6. Hemorrhoids: Hemorrhoids refer to enlarged veins in the rectal region caused by pressure from the growing uterus. Hemorrhoids can be reduced by eating a high-fiber diet, drinking lots of water, and being active.

It is important to inform your healthcare provider of any symptoms or concerns during pregnancy. While lifestyle changes can manage many common issues, in some cases, medical treatment may be required to maintain the health of both mother and baby. Most women can manage common issues during pregnancy with proper support and care. This will ensure a healthy pregnancy.

RETURNING HOME

New parents often feel overwhelmed when they return home after a stay in the hospital for labor and delivery. It is important to take care of your baby and your family during this time and be prepared for what lies ahead.

First, make sure your home is ready and safe for your arrival. You should baby-proof your home by removing sharp or dangerous objects and covering electrical outlets. You should also have all necessary baby items, such as a crib, changing table, car seat, and diapers, ready for your little one.

Understanding the emotional and physical changes that can occur following delivery is important. Postpartum can bring on discomfort, fatigue, hormonal changes, and mood swings. It is important to allow yourself to rest, recover, eat well, stay hydrated, and do gentle exercises, as directed by your healthcare provider.

Establishing a routine that works well for you and your baby is also important. This includes setting up feeding and sleeping times and deciding who will do certain tasks, such as changing diapers, feeding, or soothing your baby.

It's important to look after your baby and take care of yourself. Asking for help, asking family and friends for support, and prioritizing self-care activities like exercise, hobbies, and self-reflection are all important.

It can be exciting and rewarding to return home with a newborn baby, but it can also be challenging. New parents can make this transition smooth with support and preparation.

THE BIG DAY HAS COME

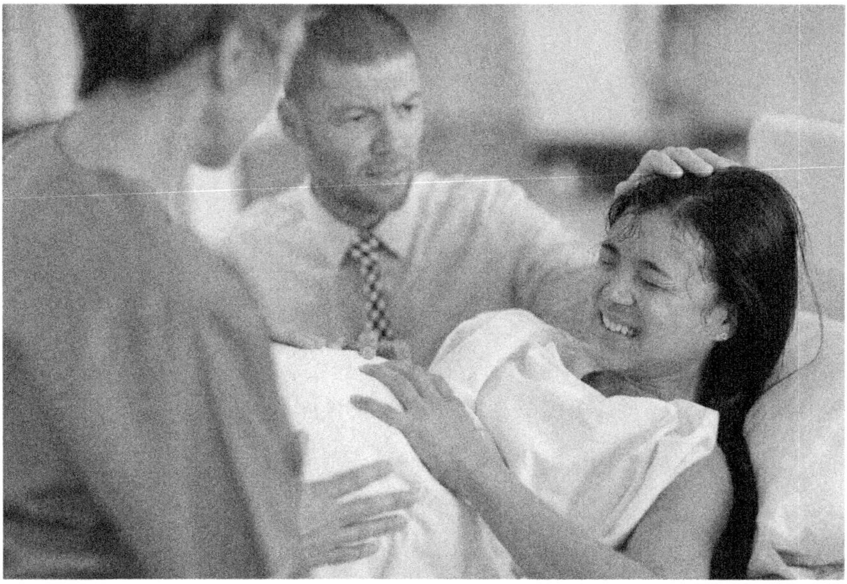

You have finally arrived at the moment you've been waiting for! You will treasure the moment of your baby's arrival for a lifetime. Although labor and delivery can seem overwhelming and intimidating, it is possible to make the process as easy as possible with some preparation. This chapter will help you understand the various stages of labor and how to support your partner. It also explains what to expect during delivery.

LABOR

The labor process refers to the sequence of events leading up to the baby's birth. It can be divided into three phases: the active or early phase, the active phase, and the transitional stage.

In the early, or latent, phase of labor, mild contractions are common. They become more frequent, regular, and stronger. During this stage, the cervix begins to dilate or efface. This phase can last hours or even days, depending on how the woman experiences it.

The active phase of labor begins when the cervix has dilated to approximately 4 cm. The contractions are more intense and frequent. The cervix continues dilation until it reaches 10 cm, at which point the baby can enter the birth canal.

The transitional phase of labor is complete when the baby's cervix has dilated to 10 cm. This is when contractions are strongest and most frequent. Mothers may feel intense sensations such as pain, pressure, and discomfort.

It is important to remain calm throughout labor. However, it is also important not to rush to the hospital. Your partner may be feeling a variety of emotions.

Traditional labor can be replaced by water birth, hypnobirthing, and acupuncture. Women can choose a home birth or a birthing center, which will provide personalized support and care throughout labor.

Many women opt for an epidural to get pain relief. This is an anesthesia that numbs your lower half. An anesthesiologist will place an epidural. It can be used to provide significant pain relief during labor.

If there are concerns or complications with the baby's health, some women may require a cesarean. This surgical procedure allows the baby to be delivered via an incision in the abdomen and uterus of the mother. This procedure is performed under general anesthesia. It can be done when it is medically necessary.

AVOID UNNECESSARY TRIPS TO THE HOSPITAL

Expectant parents can be anxious and excited about the upcoming due date. However, it is important not to make unnecessary visits to the hospital. It is important to be alert and seek medical attention when necessary. However, frequent hospital visits can be expensive and stressful for both mother and father.

False labor is a condition in which the mother-to-be experiences contractions but does not result in active labor. This is the leading reason for unnecessary hospital visits. These contractions may be painful and feel the same as active labor. False labor can happen several weeks before the due date. This could be caused by dehydration or another factor. Expectant mothers must stay hydrated and well-rested, so they don't have to go to the hospital.

False labor is not the only reason to visit the hospital. Minor injuries, mild contractions, and early signs of labor can also lead to unnecessary visits. Talking to your healthcare provider at the antenatal visit is important to address any symptoms that may require hospitalization.

You must immediately call your healthcare provider or emergency service if you experience any medical emergency, such as severe bleeding, heavy cramping, or other symptoms. Expectant parents can save money and avoid unnecessary visits to the hospital by being well-informed about when and how to seek medical attention.

STAY CALM, BUT DO NOT WAIT TOO LONG

It is important to remain calm and focused when the big day approaches. It's important not to wait to get to the hospital. The risk of complications can increase for both mother and baby if the visit is delayed.

It is important to listen to your body and not rush to the hospital. However, it is also vital to recognize signs of labor and not wait too much. Many signs indicate labor. They can include regular contractions, stronger over time, lower back pain, pressure, bloody discharge, and rupture of the amniotic capsule.

Notifying your healthcare provider if your partner experiences any of the following symptoms is important. Your healthcare provider might suggest you wait at home or go to the hospital for a checkup. Sometimes, they might recommend immediate hospitalization.

Remember that labor can be swift, and you may not have time to get to the hospital in the time necessary. It's better to be cautious and get medical advice from your healthcare provider if you're unsure if it's time for the hospital.

SUPPORT YOUR PARTNER

As a dad, it is important to support your partner through labor. Labor can be a difficult and overwhelming experience. Your partner will need all of the support she can get. These are some tips that will help you support your partner through labor.

1. Being present and attentive is the most important thing you can do for your partner. Be there for her, be with her, and give her encouragement. Pay attention to what she is saying and then respond.
2. Help your partner manage the pain. Although labor can be difficult, there are many options to help you manage it. Your partner can try pain relief techniques such as massage, breathing techniques, and cold or hot compresses. Help your partner communicate her pain to the medical staff if she takes medication.
3. You can be her advocate. Your partner might be in a vulnerable position during labor and may need someone to help her. If you are concerned about her care or feel she is not being taken care of, speak up.
4. Offer emotional support: Labor can be a rollercoaster ride, and your partner might experience various emotions. You can

listen to your partner, validate her feelings and give encouragement.

5. You can also take care of the practical aspects of labor: Communicating with your family and friends, packing bags and ensuring that you have everything you will need for your hospital stay.
6. Every labor and delivery is unique. Your partner might have special needs and preferences. Flexibility, attention, and support are key to the success of this process. This will help you and your partner have a positive, empowering birth experience.

WHAT IS LABOR ALL ABOUT?

Knowing what labor is will help expectant fathers prepare for and support their partners during childbirth. Labor is when the uterus contracts and the cervix expands to allow for the baby's birth. This is the end of nine months of labor and the beginning of parenthood.

There are three stages to labor. The contractions begin, and the cervix opens. This is the first stage. This stage, particularly for first-time mothers, can last several hours to days. Painful cramps in the back or lower abdomen often characterize this stage. This is a crucial time to support the mother-to-be by providing comfort measures and encouraging her relaxation.

The actual delivery of the baby is the second stage of labor. The baby is now free to move through the birth canal. As the baby's head emerges from the cervix, the mother may feel a strong urge to push. The rest of her body will follow. During this stage, it is important to encourage the mother.

After the baby is born, the third stage is the delivery of the placenta. This stage is typically brief and involves the delivery at the afterbirth.

It is important to remember that labor can sometimes be unpredictable and not always go according to plan. Sometimes labor can be induced or may require a cesarean section. It is important to understand the labor and delivery options and discuss them with your medical team.

Fathers are honored to be present for the birth and labor of their children. This is a chance to support the mother and welcome a new baby into the world.

LABOR - ALTERNATIVES

Expectant parents have many options when planning for their big day. Natural childbirth, water births, and of doulas or midwives are all options.

Natural childbirth is when the labor process proceeds without any medical intervention or pain medication. Relaxation techniques, breathing exercises, and other natural methods are used to manage pain and discomfort during labor. Natural childbirth is more controllable for women who choose to have it. They may feel empowered and accomplished after the birth of their baby.

Water births offer an alternative to traditional labor and delivery methods. This involves laboring in warm water and giving birth. Water birth advocates believe that water immersion can reduce pain and discomfort during labor, promote relaxation and create a supportive and gentle environment for the baby's delivery.

Midwives and doulas offer support and guidance during pregnancy and labor. Doulas provide emotional and physical support to expectant parents, while midwives can help with the baby's birth. Midwives are medical professionals. Doulas, and midwives, are great resources for expectant mothers, offering support and information throughout labor and delivery.

Regardless of your approach, it is important to talk with your healthcare provider about your options and create a birth plan that suits your needs and preferences. You can ensure you have a positive experience during labor and delivery by being prepared and well-informed.

THE PLACEMENT FOR THE EPIDURAL

An epidural is used to control pain during labor. This is a local anesthesia that numbs the lower body. It makes labor easier for mothers. An epidural injects local anesthetic via a thin, flexible tube into the epidural area in the spinal column.

An anesthesiologist (or a nurse anesthetist) will perform the procedure. They will also explain the process to the mother. A local anesthetic inserts the needle.

The epidural space is the area between the spinal cord & the spinal canal. A small needle is inserted. The needle is then passed through a tiny tube called a catheter. Once the needle has been removed, the catheter remains in place. The catheter is then inserted with the medication, which provides pain relief in 20 minutes.

You can adjust the medication to suit the needs of your mother. The catheter can also be left in place during labor. The mother will monitor any complications such as headaches or drops in blood pressure.

Although epidurals can be safe, there are some risks, such as a drop in blood pressure or fever. To make informed decisions, it is important to discuss with your healthcare provider the possible risks and benefits.

Not all epidurals are effective in pain relief. Some women may prefer alternative methods like massage, breathing exercises, and aromatherapy. It is up to the mother to decide whether or not to have an epidural.

THE ACTUAL DELIVERY

The delivery is the final step in a long and difficult journey. It marks the beginning of a new chapter in the parents' lives. Every delivery is different and may vary from person to person.

It's time for the mother to push once she reaches the delivery stage. This can take a few moments to several hours, depending on many factors, such as the mother's health or the baby's position. The medical team may guide the mother on when and how to push.

The medical team will watch the baby as they make its way down the birth canal. An episiotomy can sometimes be performed to expand the vaginal opening and and facilitate delivery.

The medical team will remove any fluid from the baby's nose and mouth and then check its overall health. The rest of the body will follow, and the baby will then be placed on the mother for skin-to skin contact. This contact is important for bonding between parents and baby as it can regulate the baby's temperature, and breathing, and helps regulate his/her body's respiration.

Mothers may feel various emotions after giving birth, such as joy, sadness, and exhaustion. As the mother adjusts to many physical and emotional changes, it is important to offer support and comfort. The medical team will monitor the mother and baby, who will also provide any medical attention needed.

Giving birth can be an exciting time for both mother and partner. It is an important step in the journey to parenthood.

ATTENTION TO THE BIRTH

It can be an unforgettable moment you will remember for the rest of of your life. Although many dads-to-be may be nervous about the process, there are some things you can do to help your partner.

Communicating with your partner and medical staff is one of the most important things you can do. You need to know your partner's wishes and the procedures of the medical staff. Ask questions, and don't be afraid of asking questions if you don't understand something.

You can provide comfort and support to your partner during labor. It is possible to make a difference by simply holding her hand, encouraging, and even providing physical support. You can ensure she is well-hydrated, give her back rubs and massages, and encourage her to change positions and move about as necessary.

The medical staff will guide how to help the baby as soon as it is born. The medical staff may ask you to cut the umbilical cord or hold your baby for the first time. Follow the directions of the medical staff. Your partner can give you guidance on how to proceed.

It's important to remember that attending a birth can be an intense and emotional experience. You are allowed to express your emotions. Many emotions can be felt during a birth: joy, awe, or even overwhelming. You should take care of your emotions and not be afraid to ask for help if you need it.

The birth of your child is an unforgettable experience. You can participate in your child's birth by communicating with your partner and providing support.

THE CESAREAN SECTION

Sometimes, a cesarean section is necessary to deliver the baby safely. This procedure involves the incision in the abdomen and uterus of the mother to deliver the baby. Your healthcare provider will inform you and your partner about the risks and benefits of this procedure.

You can be a father and play an important part in the birth process. It can be nerve-wracking, but being calm and present for your partner will help make it a more pleasant experience. These tips will help you to be supportive during pregnancy.

1. Be present: Offer encouragement and support to your partner by being in the same room as them.

2. Talk to medical personnel: Ask questions, give updates about your partner's health, and advocate for her preferences and needs.
3. Comfort: Offer comfort by using breathing techniques, massage, or other forms of physical comfort to aid your partner in coping with pain and discomfort.
4. Keep positive: Reassurance and encouragement to your partner will help you stay positive. Remind your partner of the ultimate goal: meeting your baby.
5. You should be prepared for anything: Even though you might have a birth plan, things could change rapidly during labor and delivery. You can adapt to any situation and remain positive.

Your partner must have a cesarean section. This process is more complicated than vaginal deliveries and may require additional support. Your partner may need to spend longer in the hospital.

The birth of your child can be a life-changing experience. Being present and supportive can help you support your partner during labor and delivery and get you started as parent.

The birth of your child can be both exciting and emotionally charged. You can make childbirth more enjoyable by supporting your partner, being calm during labor, and helping them to feel less alone.

HOW TO TAKE CARE OF A CHILD

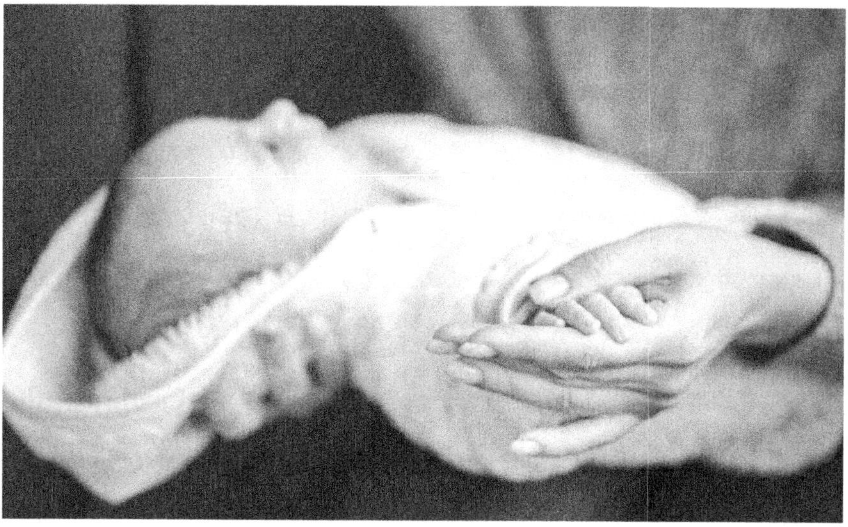

You'll face many new challenges after your baby is born. Caring for a baby involves many tasks. These include feeding, diapering, bathing, and holding it. To keep your child happy and healthy, it is important to be able to perform these tasks safely.

FEEDING A NEWBORN

For first-time parents, feeding a newborn can seem daunting. Proper nutrition is crucial for a baby's growth and development in the first few months. It doesn't matter if you breastfeed or formula feed your baby. It is important to learn the basics of breastfeeding.

Breastfeeding is the best and most natural way to feed newborns. Breastfeeding provides the best nutrition for the baby and strengthens the bond between mother, and child. Breastmilk is easy to digest and contains antibodies that may help protect your baby from illness.

You must be able to breastfeed your baby in a quiet and comfortable place. Your baby should be comfortable with their head and body aligned. It's normal for you and your baby both to take time to become comfortable with breastfeeding. Your baby might experience discomfort, and you may need to help your baby latch on.

There are many types of formula that you can choose from if your baby is formula-fed. You need to ensure that your baby can eat the right nutrition and is easy to digest. To ensure the correct mixing of the formula, you should carefully follow the directions on the packaging.

It is important to be flexible when feeding your baby. You should feed your newborn every 2-3 hours. Your baby will grow, and their eating habits will change. They will also be able to eat longer between meals.

Feeding your baby is a time of bonding. It's important to make the most of this time with your baby. You can hold your baby close and make eye contact, talk calmly to them, and breastfeed or formula feed. This is crucial for a baby's development and helps build a strong relationship between parents and children.

BREASTFEEDING

It is important to breastfeed your baby. Breastfeeding provides nutrients for your baby and boosts immunity. It promotes bonding between you, and your baby, and it also helps to strengthen your relationship with them. Here are some facts about breastfeeding.

1. Breastfeeding technique: Although breastfeeding can seem difficult to some moms, it is possible with practice. Your baby should be positioned with their head and body in line with your breast to ensure they latch on properly. Your baby should have their mouth open wide enough to cover the entire areola and not just the nipple. Your baby should to see more of the areola on the upper lip than the lower.
2. How often your baby is fed will determine how much breast milk you have. Your body will produce more milk if you give your baby more food. Breastfeeding your baby when hungry is the best way to ensure an adequate milk supply.
3. Breastfeeding has many benefits. Breast milk is rich in antibodies, which protect your baby against infections and illnesses. Breastfeeding promotes bonding between parents and babies. Breastfeeding can reduce your risk of developing certain conditions, such as breast and ovarian cancer.

4. Breastfeeding difficulties: Breastfeeding can be difficult. Some mothers might experience engorgement, sore nipples, or low milk supply. If you have difficulties breastfeeding, consult a lactation consultant or your doctor.
5. Pumping breast milk: A breast pump can be used to produce breast milk and store it later. There are many types of breast pumps, including electric and manual. You can rent a hospital-grade breast pump if you need to express milk often.

Breastfeeding is a great way to bond with your baby. Although it may take patience and practice, breastfeeding can be done with guidance and support.

CHANGING DIAPERS

New parents need to learn how to change diapers. Although it can initially seem daunting, you will soon become accustomed to changing diapers. These are some tips to get you started.

1. Make sure you have the right supplies
2. Make sure you choose a safe, clean place to change your baby. While a changing table or mat is the best, a bed or clean floor can also work.
3. Take out the dirty diaper. To take off the diaper, pull the tabs from both sides. Lift your baby's legs gently. For girls, clean the area with a damp cloth or wipes. Make sure to cover all areas.
4. The diaper is ready to go. Open the diaper and place it under the baby's bottom. The diaper's back should reach your baby's waist, while the front should touch your baby's legs.
5. Secure the diaper by bringing the front of your diaper between your baby's legs and attaching the tabs at each end. Ensure that the diaper fits comfortably but not too tightly to prevent leaks. Also, make sure the leg cuffs are securely around your legs.

6. Clean up the baby and get dressed. Use a cloth or wipes to clean the baby's bottom. Apply diaper rash cream if needed. Put the diapers and wipes away.

   It is part of daily life with a baby, and diaper changing is essential. You'll soon be comfortable with it, and you will be able to do it quickly.

BATHING YOUR BABY

It can seem daunting to bathe a newborn baby at first. But with practice, it will become less intimidating. Your baby's skin is delicate, so you should bathe them every two to three days. Too much washing can cause it to dry out. These are some ways to make bath time with your baby a success.

1. Get your supplies ready: Before bathing your baby, ensure you have everything you need. You can use mild baby soap, washcloths, towels, and a baby tub.
2. Warm water is best: Pour warm water into the bathtub. You can check the water temperature with a bath thermometer or your elbow.
3. To keep your baby warm, undress him/her.
4. Wash a washcloth with warm water. Add a little mild baby soap to the washcloth.
5. Wash your baby's skin gently with the soapy washcloth. For each eye, use a corner of the washcloth.
6. Clean your baby's skin: Use a soapy washcloth to clean their body. Start at the neck and work your way down to the feet. Be gentle, and make sure you clean all the folds.

7. Rinse and Dry: After rinsing your baby with warm water, take them out of the tub. Wrap them in a towel. Pay attention to folds and creases when drying your baby.

   Don't leave your baby alone during bath time. If your baby is undergoing a circumcision or removing the umbilical cord stump from his/her uterus, your doctor will advise you on when your baby can be bathed.

SAFELY SLEEPING

It is important to ensure that your baby gets enough sleep for their health and well-being. It's just as important to ensure that your baby is sleeping well. These are some tips that will help you make sure your baby sleeps safely.

1. Your baby should be on your back. This is the best position to sleep for them. This reduces the chance of sudden infant death syndrome (SIDS).
2. Use a firm mattress. A flat, firm surface for sleeping is the best choice for your baby. Avoid soft materials such as comforters, pillows, and stuffed animals. These can cause suffocation.
3. The crib should be free of hazards. Keep the crib clear of any toys or blankets that could distract the baby's face.
4. For the first six months to one year, it is recommended that babies share a room with their parents. This allows parents to monitor their baby's breathing better, and reduces the chance of SIDS.
5. Avoid overheating. Keep your baby's bedroom at a comfortable temperature to prevent overheating. SIDS can be increased by overheating.

6. Swaddling: While swaddling can help calm a fussy baby, it is important to do so safely. Swaddle your baby in a snug, but not too tight, covering his neck and head.
7. Use pacifiers to reduce SIDS risk: Pacifiers can be used when your baby is put to bed. It is important not to force your baby to use a pacifier if they do not want one.

These tips will help you ensure that your baby sleeps safely and comfortably. You should also remember that every baby is different and may have unique sleeping needs. Therefore, listening to your baby and adapting your approach accordingly is important.

As you can see, caring for a child is a huge responsibility. However, it's also an amazing experience. You can provide the best care by learning to properly feed, bathe, change, and hold your child. Always ensure your child's safety, well-being, and comfort.

TIME TO BE A DAD

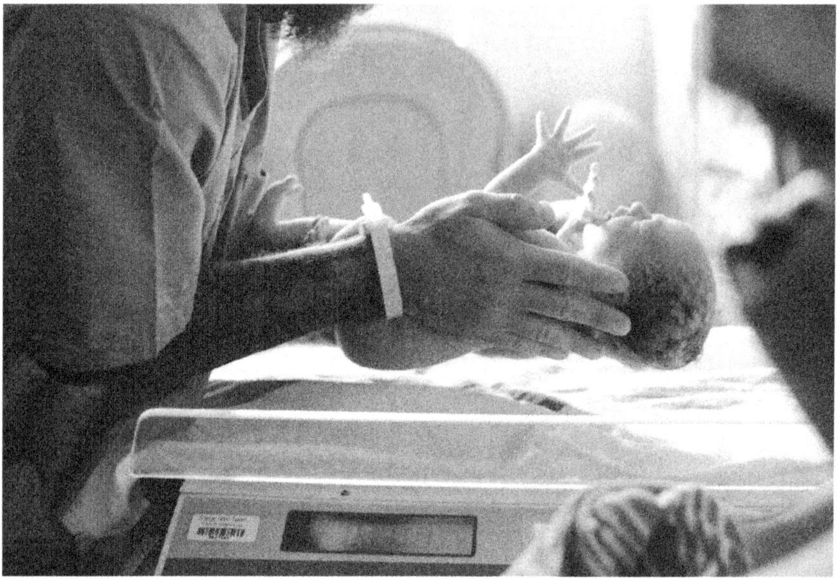

Congratulations! You are now officially a father. Your role as a parent is only beginning. There are many things you can do for your partner and your baby. This chapter will cover some important points to keep in mind as you adjust to your new dad role.

HOUSEHOLD CHOSE

You will have more responsibilities as a dad with a newborn baby. To keep your home in order, household chores are essential. These are some helpful tips to help you tackle household chores as a dad.

1. Divide the responsibilities: With your partner, sit down and create a list of all the household chores you need to do. Then divide the tasks between you. To avoid conflicts and misunderstandings, it is important to understand what each person is responsible clearly.
2. Prioritize tasks . Prioritize tasks based on their importance and urgency.
3. Flexibility is key: Your schedule and routine may need to be adjusted to meet your baby's needs. You must be flexible to meet the changing needs of parenting.
4. Make the most of your time. Use it efficiently to accomplish tasks. You can, for example, use the time your baby is taking to sleep to wash clothes or make meals.

   You can make chores more enjoyable by being creative. Make cleaning fun and involve your child in chores like folding laundry.

   Take care of your home together.

PREPARING MEALS

Helping to cook meals is one way to support your partner as a dad. For new mothers, a healthy, balanced diet is crucial for their recovery, breastfeeding, and energy. It is also important for dads to ensure that their children receive the right nutrients during this crucial time.

Although it may seem daunting to prepare meals, there are simple steps you can take to make it easier. Start by planning, making a shopping list, and then grocery shopping with your partner. This will not only save you time and energy, but it also lets you choose healthy and nutritious food for your family.

Consider simple, healthy, and easy recipes when preparing your meals. For convenience, you can prepare meals ahead of time and keep them in the freezer or fridge. You can also prepare meals that are easy to reheat, such as stews or curries and roast vegetables.

You should also consider your partner's dietary preferences and restrictions, especially if you are breastfeeding. Certain foods can cause discomfort or allergic reactions in babies, so limiting or avoiding them is important. You can consult a nutritionist to ensure your baby and partner are well-fed.

It's not about the cooking; it's about supporting your family and partner. You are setting an example for your children by taking part in the kitchen.

NOW PRESENT

It's crucial to be involved as a father, especially if you're a first-time dad. This includes being present for your partner throughout the pregnancy, attending medical appointments, and being involved in your baby's care and feeding.

Being present does not only mean being physically present in the same room with your baby and partner but also mentally and emotionally present. This involves actively listening to your partner's and baby's needs and responding promptly and appropriately.

It is important that you take an active part in caring for your baby during the first few weeks. You will need to learn how to bathe, change diapers, and feed your baby. This is true whether you're breastfeeding your baby or helping your partner. Your partner can take over household chores like cleaning, cooking, and laundry so that they can focus on bonding and recovering with their baby.

Being present means supporting your partner through the postpartum period. Many new mothers experience emotional and physical symptoms, such as anxiety, exhaustion, mood swings, and anxiety. Your role as a support person is to listen to and offer emotional support.

Being present is about acknowledging that you are an important part of your child's life. Your child will look up to you for support and guidance throughout their growth. Being involved with your child is important and it can also prove rewarding for you.

SUPPORT HER DURING BREASTFEEDING

Breastfeeding your baby is a healthy and natural way to give them the necessary nutrients. Breastfeeding can be overwhelming for new mothers. You, as a father, play an important role in encouraging and supporting your partner while breastfeeding.

It is important to be educated about breastfeeding to support your partner. You can learn about breastfeeding and how to latch your baby properly. This information will help you better understand and support your partner.

It is important to offer support and encouragement. Breastfeeding can be difficult and exhausting. Your partner might feel discouraged or overwhelmed at times. Let your partner know you are there for them and appreciate all the work she has put into breastfeeding.

You should also be practical and assist with breastfeeding tasks. You can assist with things like changing diapers, burping, and fetching water for the baby. You can take some pressure off her and make breastfeeding easier.

Be patient and understanding. Breastfeeding takes time. Mother and baby both need to be patient. Encourage your partner and remind her about the benefits of breastfeeding.

It is important to listen to your partner during breastfeeding. You may find it difficult to breastfeed in public. Be supportive and understanding of her wishes to have a private place to do so. You can carry a cover or shawl to protect your baby while she is feeding.

Being a dad is all about supporting your partner while breastfeeding. You can ensure your partner has a successful and positive breastfeeding experience by being patient, educated, practical, supportive, and patient.

COMMON PROBLEMS

Being a dad is not an easy task. Many issues can arise in the postpartum period. Sleep deprivation is one of the most common problems. Parents often have to be awake at night for newborns. This can lead to sleep deprivation. It is important to find ways to manage fatigue, such as taking turns caring for the baby and taking naps whenever possible.

Stress and feeling overwhelmed are other common problems. A new dad may feel under pressure to care for their children, do household chores, and be a good father. Communicate with your partner, share responsibilities, and seek support from family, friends, and a support group.

Feelings of isolation and disconnection from children or partners can also be a problem for new dads. A new baby can emphasize the mother and her needs. It is easy for fathers to feel neglected or insignificant. Communicate your concerns and feelings with your partner. Find ways to bond with your child by taking them on a walk, reading to them, and doing other activities.

Holding the baby for too long or doing household chores can cause physical symptoms like back pain, shoulder pain, or fatigue. These symptoms can be relieved by engaging in light exercise, stretching, and receiving a massage from your partner.

It is important to recognize signs of depression after a baby. New parents can experience anxiety, sadness, and mood swings. If these symptoms persist or become more severe, it's important to seek professional assistance. Postpartum depression can affect both parents. It can be treated with medication or counseling.

It can be not easy to become a dad. However, acknowledging common problems, finding support, and communicating with your partner will help you navigate this new chapter in your life with ease and confidence.

PHYSICAL SYMPTOMS

Postpartum can be difficult for new moms. Physical symptoms can play a major role in that process. Mothers need to rest after giving birth. Many physical symptoms can be experienced, and each woman may have different symptoms.

Fatigue is one of the most common symptoms that new mothers experience. Mothers can feel exhausted from caring for newborns around the clock. This can leave them feeling tired and in desperate need of some rest. Many women feel tired and uncomfortable in their perineal region, making it difficult to sit and walk. This may be more severe in women who have had an episiotomy or were required to use forceps during childbirth.

Breast engorgement is another common symptom after a baby's birth. Breast engorgement can occur when a mother's milk is introduced to her breasts. This can make breastfeeding difficult. Further discomfort and pain can be caused by engorgement, obstructed ducts or mastitis.

Women who have had a baby may experience hair and skin changes. Some women may experience acne, dry skin, or skin discoloration. Some women may experience hair loss in the months after delivery.

Some women may experience bleeding or discharge postpartum, which can last up to six weeks after giving birth. This is known as lochia and comprises blood, mucus, and uterine tissue.

New dads need to be aware and offer support to their wives. To help new moms recover and rest, dads can take on more household chores and baby care duties. If their partner is experiencing severe symptoms or difficulty caring for their newborn, dads should encourage them to seek medical attention.

RECONNECTING POSTPARTUM DEPRESSION

Some mothers suffer from postpartum depression after giving birth. This is a serious mental condition that can impact not only the mother but the entire family. New mothers commonly feel overwhelmed and emotional after giving birth, but postpartum depression requires immediate attention.

Postpartum depression can manifest as feeling depressed, empty, and hopeless for a prolonged period. It can also cause changes in your appetite, and sleep patterns and loss of interest in things that once brought joy. Mothers may have thoughts about harming their baby or themselves in severe cases.

Recognizing these symptoms is crucial, as contacting a healthcare provider immediately. Healthcare providers can offer support and therapy, including medication or therapy. Partner support is also essential since postpartum depression does not come as a choice.

Not only is it important to remember that postpartum depression may occur anytime during the first year after the birth but also in the weeks following the delivery. Partners should be supportive and attentive even after the first postpartum period.

Postpartum depression can be treated with medical treatment. Lifestyle changes are also possible to help. These include sleeping enough, exercising, eating healthy, and spending quality time with family members.

New parents must be aware of the possibility of postpartum depression and seek treatment if necessary. New mothers can overcome this condition with proper support and treatment. They can also enjoy their new role as parents.

GET BACK TO HAVING SEX

Many couples notice a decline in sexual activity after the birth of a baby. This is normal and can be explained by the emotional and physical changes both parents experience during pregnancy, labor, and delivery. New dads must understand that intimacy is an essential component of a healthy relationship. However, it is possible to go back to having sex.

It is important to be patient and slow down. It may take some time before your partner feels comfortable again engaging in sexual activity. Be supportive and let your partner know you are there to support her.

You should also communicate with your partner about any changes in your physical or emotional health since you became a parent. Sleep deprivation, stress, and physical exhaustion can impact sexual desire and function. Talking about these issues openly can help you feel more at ease and in tune with one another.

Slowing down and paying attention to your partner's comfort is important. Start with non-sexual forms such as hugging, cuddling, and kissing. You can slowly progress to sexual activity as your partner gets more comfortable. Do not rush and listen to your partner.

Safe sex is important, and you should take steps to avoid pregnancy until you're ready to have another baby. To prevent unintended pregnancies, condoms and other forms of birth control are essential.

It's important that you remember that sex after having children may not be the same as before. It may take time for your partner to adjust to the changes in their body. To ensure a happy, healthy, and fulfilling sexual relationship, it is important to be patient, open-minded, and communicative.

CONCLUSION

Being a father can be a life-changing experience. It requires patience, preparation, and willingness to learn. You will experience joys and challenges as you become a father, from the moment you hear you are going to be one until the day you welcome your baby home.

This book covers everything you need to know regarding pregnancy, and childbirth, and how to care for your child. We've discussed what changes to expect in your professional and personal lives, how to babyproof your home, and how to deal with the first, second, and third trimesters.

We've discussed the medical complications that can arise during pregnancy.

We also discussed the various aspects of labor and birth, including how to prepare for it and how to attend birth.

It is important to remember that you're not alone on this journey. You have your partner, family, friends, and medical professionals there to help you when you need it.

It is important to recognize that fathers have a shared responsibility for caring for their children. This is not the job of just the mother, but both parents must be involved in raising their child. This means sharing the household chores, cooking meals, and supporting your partner while you breastfeed.

You should also recognize and treat any emotional and physical symptoms you or your partner might be experiencing. Many mothers experience postpartum depression, which is common. It is important to seek treatment if you have any symptoms.

It is important to remember that intimacy is essential to any healthy relationship. It can be difficult to get back to sex after childbirth. However, patience, communication, and understanding will help you overcome all obstacles.

The journey to fatherhood requires patience, love, and the willingness to learn. We hope this book has prepared you for this amazing experience. We wish you every success as a dad.